SELF- HELP : HOW TO BE INVINCIBLE : A SHORT PRATICAL GUIDE FOR A HAPPY POSITIVE LIFE

TABLE OF CONTENTS

INTRODUCTION :

Sometimes life gets really hard, and it starts slowly infecting your mental health. You feel depressed, anxious, in pain and panic. And no one really understands what you are going through because those feelings are isolating you from the whole world. When everyone is sleeping, you are awake. And when everyone is awake, you are sleeping. You want to talk to someone, but you feel like your voice is refusing to get out because your heart is broken and the pain is unspeakable. We can't change life and people. We can't stop them from hurting us. However, we can change ourselves to be less affected by it ups and downs. Life is not always pink. Sometimes, it kicks us really hard. We have to train ourselves to raise quickly after the fall and not remain on the ground depressed for years. So, you have to be flexible in order to survive from people and life kicks.

The reason I wrote this book is that I don't want you to waste your time in depression. I don't want the bad times to prevent you from living the good times. Because unconsciously, we are giving sadness the biggest part in our lives. The good moment makes us happy for a second but the bad moment makes us sad for a century. Even the thing that we are afraid of in the future, we are worried about from now. You are destroying your present by some unreal events created in your own head that can't even happen. We have to be stabilised. Unfortunately, we are created to be happy, but we are learning to be sad. Life is too short. It's a moment. So benefit from the good times. And if you don't have them, create them.

In this tiny book, I'm going to help you build a happy person from the inside and be invincible. I experienced every single word in this book, and I want to help you with this experience. It was such a long and tough journey, but it was worth it because I learned a lot of things and it made me see things differently. I wish I can help you too with this book. I'm just like you. I survived and I promise you that you will survive too. Now, I'm going to give you the keys to be invincible.

1- MENTAL HEALTH :

Our mental health is critical. But, we are not giving it any importance. We keep sacrificing it for some material things and wasting it. Then, the endless pain starts. It feels like taking your soul out of your body again and again. You feel dead, but you are alive. If you are already feeling bad right now. I'm just going to tell you one thing. It's normal to feel sad and weak. It's normal to cry, but those tears will fix nothing, even when you cry for days. You will only end up with puffy eyes. You are sad because you have problems in your life. You need to think and try to solve them. If you are in a game right now. What are you going to do? Are you going to quit the game and start crying? Of course not, you will try harder until you win. What's the difference? You are being too sensitive in the real life. Sometimes, we need to be cool and less serious in order to solve our problems. You can pretend it's a game because those negative feelings are the biggest obstruction. You can't think wisely with this toxic fog in your head and those hot tears in your eyes. I know those feelings are so strong but you have to try to get out of this bad situation. I'm going to shock you right now. Most of your bad feelings are fake. They are coming from overthinking. You have a problem. Instead of thinking of a solution, you make it bigger and bigger until your head blows up. For example, I have problem A. It can cause problem B and if I have the B, I can easily have the C and the D… then, all the alphabets. Problem A is the real one and the others are fake. You are only exaggerating and complicating things.

You only created them to cause yourself anxiety. Do you love being anxious and depressed ?

I guess not. The other thing is thinking about the past and relate it with the future. If I failed in the past, I will also fail in the future. If I was sad, I will be always sad. You are judging your future as if it was a curse, and it's following you until you die. There is no relation between your past and your future. I know that past failure really hurts and the hardest part that you can't find any explanation. Why this happens to me? Why I keep failing? I don't deserve it. Well, you deserve it because it was a precious lesson for special people like you. You become stronger, more patient, smarter. Pain is the best chance to change your entire life when you take it as a stimulant, not as a barrier. It can make up for all those tough years that you think you wasted in pain. Actually, you lost nothing. You gained a lot of wisdom that can make you achieve a twenty-year success in just two years. Pain gives you the biggest power because it's provocative and it pushes you forward with a very high speed. For example, you are in a race with many people. While everyone reaches the middle of the road, you are still in the beginning. Then, a dog attacks you and starts biting you. Are you going to remain in your place and give up? Of course not, you are going to run away from the dog. Why? because it was so painful and threatening. And thanks to that dog, you are going to run faster and you will reach the end before the others because they are comfortable; they are not chased by a dog and they didn't feel the pain. It really wakes you up and excites you. When you are in danger, you will give the highest potential and you will do unbelievable things. This is how miracles are made. This is how legends are made. They came from pain.

Also, there is something else in order to save your mental health is to learn to ignore. You don't have to concentrate on everything. In some cases, the best way to deal with them is just to ignore them. It's not even worth your time or your effort. If you focus on everything, you will end up in the madhouse. You don't have to give attention to everything, to everyone and to every word. Try to control your feelings and your reactions. Just be cool and move on. It's ok to have a different point of view. It's doesn't mean we are enemies. When you accept the differences in everything, you will be more peaceful. Also, you have to ignore everything that hurts you. If you are not comfortable in a place, leave it. If someone keeps causing you pain, get him out of your life. Don't hesitate because you will be messing with your mental health. Or, you will definitely pay for your concessions with a lot of mental diseases. Always try to protect yourself from all the toxic things in life.

2- SATISFACTION :

I know it's hard, but you have to accept your current situation no matter how bad it is. Rule number 1, if you want to change it, accept it first. Stop focusing on the bad things or the things that you don't have. Focus instead on the good things you have, even the little things that you think they are not important. For example, your health, your family, your bed, your food, your water, the little money you earn. I can hear you saying everyone have them, it's not a big deal. Well, I don't agree with you. First, think for a second about the homeless, people suffering from famine and wars. Second, if I starve or dehydrated you, you will definitely die. But I'm sure you will survive without the Ferrari that you are driving in your dreams. Believe me, as long as you are not satisfied, you are going to drive it only in your head.

Start counting your blessings, appreciate them, and thank God for them. If you thank him, he will give you more. Also, satisfaction is a relieving feeling. It gives you peace, tranquility and a strong positive energy. It clears your mind from all the stressful negative thoughts. And at that moment, you will start thinking better, creating positive thoughts, finding solutions, making plans and seeing things clearly. Just take a rest. You are sinking from the inside and you can't change anything with hate and rejection. Satisfaction is like your pillars and you are like a building. If your pillars are weak, you will definitely fall even when you become a huge building with many achievements. That's why sometimes successful people having everything in life: money, popularity, beauty, fans, commit suicide. When we hear that, we get shocked « why they did that? They have everything!!! ». Yes, it's true. They build themselves very high but they forget the most important thing the strong pillars. So, if you are still a small building or you built nothing yet. Congratulations, it will be much easier for you because you are still in the beginning. So, build strong pillars first. Then build yourself. And, a strong one floor house is better than a weak skyscraper.

How to accept ?

Just take a look at the people that their cases are much worse than yours : the homeless, the poor, the sick. The people losing the real important things in life. The four blessings : health, food, water, shelter. Try to visit a charity or a hospital. You will be surprised. You will find them thankful because losing those real blessings makes you realise how important they are or how small the other things are. The things that you are dying for, that destroying you, stopping your life and making you sad. They are just minors. Don't let the world misleads you. They are easy and achievable comparing to your health that you are about to ruin it for them. Depression is killing you. So stop it. You don't need any medication or sedatives. You are fine. All you need is to be calm, grateful. After that, you will achieve all the things that you want. Satisfaction doesn't mean laying down and watching things falling apart. It means I accept it but I'm going to change it. It's the first step to change.

3- LOVE YOURSELF :

Please love yourself for no reason because everyone is looking for a reason to love you. Don't treat yourself the way others treat you. Give yourself some mercy, some warmth. Be your own shelter. Confort yourself, embrace it and tell her I will always love you unconditionally. We are all looking for that person who loves us, no matter how flowed we are. Be that person and stop looking on the outside. It's all inside you. If you love and accept yourself. You will never care, even if the entire world hates you. Stop that war between you and yourself. Live in peace with yourself. If you don't love yourself, how do you expect others to love you.

Look in the mirror. Look right in your eyes, in your soul. Can you see the way they are shining ? Now, say « I am beautiful and I love myself the way I am. I don't care if no one thinks that because I think that. I can feel it and the only opinion that matters is mine. It's my face. It's my body. It's my life. » Don't wait for them to say it, say it to yourself. You deserve all the love and compliments. Don't judge yourself according to their stupid beauty standards that change every single year. You are not a product. You are a human being. I don't want you to be obsessed with those beauty trends because it will make you crazy trying to fit them by doing endless plastic surgeries.

I am not against it if you have a congenital defect distorting your face. But, nowadays, It's getting crazy. They are changing their body shapes in order to be like some fake models by removing their ribs and putting toxic implants in their bodies. It's painful and dangerous. Or by following strict diets that can lead to anorexia or bulimia. Beauty is about being healthy and comfortable. For example, you want to lose weight. First, accept your body the way it is. It will make less pressure on you, and it will lead to better results. Second, try to follow a plan in order to fix this problem. In this case, try to exercise regularly and follow a healthy diet. You can get rid of the sweets and the junk food and replace it with vegetables and fruits. But the most important thing that you don't put a pressure on yourself. Just be comfortable in your own skin and improve yourself step by step. « **God created the human being in the best design.** » This is a true fact and it means you are already perfect just the way you are even without trying. Being different dosn't mean you are ugly. It means you are special.

4- BREAK THE CURSE OF ATTACHMENT :

It's out of your control. You can't deal anymore with your problems, your fears and your insecurities. At this point, you are going to choose the easiest option. You will decide to run away from yourself trying to find solution and peace in the outside by looking for people to help you. But, remember, weak persons only attract toxic people to their lives who want to take advantage of you. He is not going to mend your broken pieces. If your life is a mess, don't get in a relationship because there are only two possibilities. The first one, you will meet the good person and he is going to help you in the beginning. But, then, Your negative energy will start invading him and he will probably leave you in order to survive. The second one which is the most common case. You will meet the toxic person who feeds on weak people and who wants to destroy the left pieces of your life. At first, he is going to pretend that he loves you and wants to help you. And when he makes sure that you are deeply attached to him, he will start hurting you, ignoring you and manipulating you. But, the worst part is in both cases, you are cursed by the sick attachment. It's more like drug addiction. You can't continue your life without that person. He will become your whole world. You can't get rid of him even when you know he is bad, or the relationship is not working. It's hurting you but you are going on anyway.

It's so hard and painful to break that curse. So, you have better watch yourself from the beginning. Don't fall in love if you are broken, fragile and your life is a mess because you will find yourself in the attachment corner which is not even love, it's a disease. You are going to live under the mercy of a human being. And humans are not perfect. Sometimes, they are bad, rude, busy.... And you are spending the whole day nervous, on the other side of the line, waiting for a text, a call, a word, a compliment, an answer, a solution, a hope, a love.... Waiting for someone to show you that you deserve to be loved because you think you don't deserve love and you don't even love yourself. Waiting for someone to fix you because you are unable to fix yourself and your problems.

You are attached to them because you are empty from the inside. You don't know how to love yourself, how to take care of yourself. You are a lost soul floating in the universe. Go get your soul back in your body. Lock yourself in a room, in a house. I don't care, even for days. You have to be alone. I know it's hard because you are afraid of yourself, your feelings and your past. Talk to yourself. Try to understand your feelings, your needs, your fears, your insecurities, your goals and your dreams. You can write them if you want. Don't run away from yourself, face it. You have to or you will explode into depression, anxiety and sick attachment. Treat it like a little child and tell her, « I understand you. Don't be afraid. I'm with you and I will treat you better. I promise you I will make you happy and help you achieve your dreams, no matter how impossible they are. »

What should I do if I'm already attached to someone ?

Let me tell you from the start that it is difficult, but you have to do it. You have no choice, especially when the other person is abusing you. Try to lock tightly all the doors between you and the other person. You have to be brave to do it. Deactivate temporarily all your social media accounts. Trust me, you will feel so comfortable after that. Change your number or you can just add his number to the blacklist. If he is living in the same town and he knows your address. If it's hard for you to move to another place. When he comes to your house, never open the door for him. Try to avoid the places where he goes. The most important thing is that you have to make yourself busy because emptiness makes you easily attached to others. Find a job, work harder, go to the gym, meet your friends, travel even to another state at a low cost, help others... You have to fill your life. If the person you are attached to is a psycho and start stalking you, threating you or hitting you. Just call the police.

And remember, you don't need anyone to complete you. You are already completed and you have all the abilities to survive. When you learn to be happy on your own from the inside, you will make others happy, attract positive people to your life, and get involved in healthy successful relationships.

Also, being attached to your goals and giving them a big importance is a nasty habit. Especially when you feel like you can't live without it or you will not be happy unless you have it. This will drudge up feelings of worry, fear, anger, sadness. And those negative feelings of resistance will stop you from achieving your goals. Also, when you put a condition to be happy, you will never be happy. For example, you say « I will be happy if I get that job. » Even after getting the job, you are still not happy because you will find yourself unconsciously putting another condition of happiness. You will say next « I will be happy if I get that car. » And in the end, you will notice that you spent your life trying to fill a long list of tasks in order to be happy and you are not even happy. Why are you complicating things? It's so simple. You don't have to climb a mountain to be happy. You can be happy even when you are down because happiness is just a feeling. All you have to do is to allow yourself to be happy because it is all in your head and those conditions are created by your brain to make it harder for you. Just relax and switch on the happiness button. Being happy anyway and letting go everything by not giving them importance will attract your goals and your desires. Start by being happy and then all your dreams will come to you.

5- STOP PLAYING THE VICTIM ROLE :

Life is hard. I know that sometimes everything become against you. Bad conditions, people putting you down, even your health is letting you down and you feel like you can't take it anymore. So, you decide to take a step back. You are shocked something must be wrong. Then, you start crying, trying to take sympathy from the world, and you realize that this is your fate. You are chosen for the victim's role in this life. After some time, your features, your posture, your acts and your words will speak for you, saying you are miserable. The people around you, will easily notice how miserable you are. I guess you are happy now. You made it; you are seeking sympathy from them. But here's the good news, they will make you more miserable because you are acting like a pathetic victim. Your terrible life will become worse.

As long as you are a prey, you will always attract hunters. If you are sad, life will make you more sad.

You are not a deer; they are not lions and it's not the jungle. We are all humans and we have the same abilities. You think they are stronger than you because they have money, popularity, muscles. Well, this is not the real power. The real power is in our brains. We are all have 100 billion cells in our brains. So, what's your excuse ?

Stop making excuses and stop telling those boring sad stories to every person you meet and especially to yourself. Because it was past and it is over now. Telling it again and again and bringing those deadly feelings to life are holding you back. We are all have some bad chapters in our lives. We don't have to live it again and again because it will come a day when you are running out of empty papers. Your book will end, and at this moment you will realize that you are rewriting the same sad events, and you are locked in the same sad zone in your entire life. But it's too late. If you don't want to get to that point, bring your past back and face it for the last time. And say « It happened, and it's over. I'm not running away from you. I'm accepting you. It's ok to have dark times in our lives. It's part of the story. Pain strengthened me. I'm proud of myself. I survived and I have new happy chapters to write. »

When people harm you or put you down or tell you that you can't do it, the best revenge is to just ignore them and succeed. Don't let them control your life or your future or your mood. You are the king or the queen of your life. If you let them stop you, you are the only one who's going to lose. They are not going to lose anything. While they are happy, you are sad. Who wins ? of course they win. You are only helping them destroying yourself. You are proving they are right and giving them the chance to see what they want to see. You are only torturing yourself. You are killing yourself because they want to see you dying. But you want to be alive. So, fight and don't let anyone steal your dreams. Protect your dreams because they are your only treasure. You are living for them. Face the people that want to stop you and tell them « No, not me ! » with a cold blood, a dark silence and a mocking smile. Come down and relax. It's just a toxic cloud passing by. There is a proverb says « People will throw stones at you, don't throw them back. Collect them and build an empire. » Don't waste your time with hate, grudge and anger because they will ruin your inner peace and distract you from your goals. And this type of people don't deserve your precious time. They don't deserve a place in your mind. Move on, you have more important things in your life. And if you want to forget them and get rid of their negative energy, forgive them. It's not for them, it's for your inner peace. Because only forgiveness and focusing on your dreams will make you succeed.

6- CONFIDENCE :

Confidence is the secret of success. When you decide to do something with a low self-esteem, you will definitely fail even if you have all the tools to do it. Confidence makes you overcome all the obstacles by not giving up and trying harder. The world is like your echo. If you believe in yourself and say « I can do it. » the world's response will be « yes you can do it and I will help you to do it. » Then, you will notice that your road become paved and the people become helpful. On the other hand, if you say « I can't do it. » the world will say « sure you can't do it. » Your road become more winding and the people become meaner. You will lose a lot if you are not confident because your reality is a reflection of your feelings. Confidence makes your path easier and shorter. Your thoughts, your feelings and your self-image are controlling indirectly your results. If you believe in yourself, you are already walked 70% of your path.

Where confidence comes from ?

We are all born confident. But, as we grow up the society, family, friends start ruining our confidence by saying wrong affirmations about us such as you are ugly, you are stupid ; you are bad ; you are a loser.... Unconsciously, we take their toxic ideas about us as facts. We get used to the nasty habit of knowing ourselves through them. We stock them in our heads as a description of ourselves. Then, we start acting according to those fake informations till we make them real. So, all you have to do is to blow up those wrong informations about you. Rediscover the real you. Back in our childhood, we couldn't do anything about it. We were immature and we took all the informations from the outside. Now, as we grow up, we have to stop acting like Childs. We have to filter all the informations coming from the others. It's not that other human who's going to show you who you are, no matter how close he is or how wise he is. He can't be closer than you to yourself. People are not your mirror. When you look at them, you see yourself. Your mirror is inside you. If you don't know yourself very well and you don't know your abilities, your qualities, your flaws, the description of yourself in your head will be empty. And unconsciously, you will start filling it with wrong information coming from the others. This means if you are smart and you don't know that, it's not written in your head and people tell you « you are stupid », you are going to take this information and you are going to act like a dumb one for the rest of your life.

It’s like your manual. You have to write it by yourself or you will always be lost, shaky, fragile and this where low self-esteem comes from. Even your flaws, you have to know them and accept them. Because if you keep ignoring them and someone tells you your flaw, you will be shocked and you will start refusing it. Then, you will become sad with a low self-esteem. And sometimes, people tend to exaggerate. They will make your flaw look bigger than what really is, and this is going to make your situation much worse. So, in order to avoid all of this and save your mental health, you have to know your flaws and accept them. It’s your field against all the bullies. For example, if someone calls you fat and you are refusing that, you will feel really hurt. This can even lead to a depression. But, if you accept it, « it’s ok, I gained some weight. » After that, even if the whole world calls you fat, you will be neutral because you are already protected yourself. It’s like a vaccine. You have to take it to protect yourself from people's diseases. And always remember, you can fix everything. It’s never too late. It’s never impossible. You have to focus on your qualities and praise them. Make your flaws look smaller in order to fix them. Don’t you ever exaggerate.

When you gain some weight, don’t say I’m ugly. When you fail at anything in your life, don’t say I’m a loser. Beware of what you are saying because your subconscious mind will believe you and take this as a reality.

The other reason for low self-esteem is comparison. It's absolutely destructive. You can easily go from ten to zero in one second just by checking social media applications. The perfect photos, the photo-shopped bodies and faces, their super family and partners, their luxury life. I'm not offending them, but most of them are fake and filters are no longer a secret. Even if their perfect life is real, it doesn't make you any smaller. So, stop cursing yourself and your life. Don't compare yourself to anyone. You are original, even if no one in this earth knows that because the important opinion about you is yours. And nothing in this world is worth your mental health, your self-esteem and your inner peace, nor the cars or the diamonds or the muscles or the people. You are exceptional. You are different. You are not like them. You don't have to be like them because no one has to be like anybody else. We don't have to be similar. If you want to progress, don't put other people as goals. You have to build a better version of yourself in your mind and put it as a goal. And always compare yourself to the older you. After some time, you will notice that you are improving.

Comparing yourself with others is only holding you back, killing you from the inside, making you hopeless and insecure and distracting you from your goals. Your brain is created for you to improve your life. So, don't fill it with other people's lives. They have their own brains working for them. They don't need you. While they are living their lives, you are wasting yours, sitting in the back seats watching them, cursing your life, your face, your body, your family, counting their qualities and forgetting yours. Don't be surprised. Of course you have qualities. Everyone has. But the difference between you and the perfect people that you are impressed with them, is confidence. They were confident even when they had nothing. They believed in themselves when no one did. They appreciated their qualities and worked on them to be that perfect. And after that, the whole world begin to believe on them because it's all start from you. While they are supporting themselves, you are acting like an ennemy. You are your worst ennemy by being unconfident. You are blocking yourself by believing you are inferior and treating yourself like a trash everyday. Aren't you tired from being one of the crowd ? Aren't you tired of being your ennemy ? Aren't you tired from the backseats ? You are created for a reason. You are created to do not to watch them do. You have to believe in you and talk to yourself positively everyday. Treat it like your loved one. If you have nothing good to say to yourself. Lie but you have to believe in those lies. « I'm beautiful, i'm strong, i'm great, i'm special... » Your subconcious mind is blind but so powerful. He believes everything you say even unreal things and he makes it real. Those positive lies will become your truth. Don't wait for the others to believe on you because they only believe when they see. And belief is the acceptance that something exists without any proof. So, you have to do it by yourself because it's something personal. Belief will give you the greatest power and no one can ever defeat you.

7- FREE FROM SOCIETY CONTROL :

Society is manipulating us in a very smoothy way that we can't even know about it. The way we act, the way we wear, even our dreams. This makes us under their pressure because we are all afraid of being judged. We want always to keep our brilliant social image. I can't deny that it feels great to be loved by everyone, but the problem is, it's impossible. You are just killing yourself for nothing. You are thinking a lot before you talk, wearing like they want, acting like they want. And you are not even going to please them. They are going to criticize you, anyway. People's satisfaction is unreachable purpose. And even if the whole world starts loving you. Where are you in all of that ?

It's your life. Do the things that you want. Why are you doing that ?

You are acting like they want because you want to hear what you want. You are beautiful; you are kind; you are sweet.... You look happy to hear that but from the inside those words are suffocating you because they are obliging you to give them more: more of your time, more of your dreams, more of saying yes. This stupid role you are taking to please them, but you didn't think of yourself. You are sacrificing your life and your dreams for them. You don't even exist in your own life. You are hurting yourself to please them. Take off that silly mask and be yourself. Let me tell you one thing: do whatever you want as long as you are not harming anyone. Don't be afraid because you will regret it at the end of your life and you will realize that you waste it. Always ask yourself What I Want? And do I really want that? You don't have to act like your friends or your siblings. If they get married at an early age, don't squeeze yourself to be like them or you will find yourself with the wrong person. If you are not ready for something, don't do it. Don't be ashamed of who you are. Maybe you have another plan or other dreams. Don't just go with the flow. Also, putting yourself in the last place and trying to satisfy everyone will make people treat you like a mop. They will wipe their dust with you. When you get dirty, they will throw you. It's not their fault. You made them selfish. So, when someone asks you for something and you feel uncomfortable to do it, just say no. Don't be afraid of being yourself and the person who truly loves you will accept you the way you are. So, you are not going to lose anything because those people who they left you for being yourself didn't love you from the beginning. If you want to please everyone, you will lose yourself. Now, I'm going to give you a spell. The most magical words « I don't care! » You don't have to say it, just feel it. If I act this way, that person will think I'm rude. « I don't care! » I really don't want to wear make up today but I'm afraid they will think ugly. « I don't care! » See, it's simple. As long as you are polite and not hurting anyone, you can use that spell.

8- GET OUT OF YOUR COMFORT ZONE :

What's the most comfortable place in your house ?

The couch, the bed, even if it colors faint or becomes older. The iron springs protrude through the mattress and stab you with their sharp ends. It's a bad situation but you still comfortable there for two reasons. First, you get used to these severe conditions. Second, you don't have the courage to change it. After you check out the couches prices, you will say « it's too expensive. I can't afford it, and there's no way to make more money. » Then, you will start looking for excuses by convincing yourself that your bad situation is good. You will say « What's wrong with this old couch. It's great and comfortable. Those painful springs make it more fun to set there. It new color is more vibrating and matches more the curtains. Wait a minute, what if the other couch is less comfortable ? I'm scared to change... » Don't be panic, it's not only your problem. It's everyone problem and there where comes the comfort zone. Humans find comfort in stability. Change shakes their brains, especially when it comes to changing habits, jobs, people, making fateful decisions. The big problem is that you don't even know whether your current situation is good or bad because you are comfortable, anyway. You become completely blind and you are creating foolish excuses to convince yourself that you are seeing clearly your situation. What if you are feeling comfortable in a hell and you are refusing to get out of it because it's simply your comfort zone ? Sometimes our brains and our feelings trick us. You can't rate your life objectively because of the comfort zone. So, I'm going to give you a trick. If your life was a movie and you are watching it now on a screen. What do you think of it ? Is it a bad or a good movie or do you find it a little boring ? What do you think about you as the main character ? Is he controlling his life and trying to change or his life is controlling him ?

If you find it an awful movie and the main character is just going with the flow and doing nothing about it. Then, I'm sorry to tell you that you are stuck in your comfort zone. And it's horrible. You have to change it now. You say « I'm afraid and it's hard. » Your feelings are normal because to pass from a situation to another, you have to make an effort and experience the feelings of discomfort, fear and insecurity. It's like moving from a comfortable island to an unknown island. You have to swim to get there and it can be dangerous, but I'm sure it's less dangerous than staying paralysed in your place. You have to take the risk and believe me, it's worth it. As long as you get to the other island, you will feel uncomfortable at first because it's a strange place for you. But then, you will be comfortable again. So, to upgrade to a higher level, you have to be courageous and not afraid of change. Don't be a comfort zone slave. Fight those fake feelings of fear and discomfort that chain you. I'm not asking you to build an empire. Start by making little changes in your life. Change some bad habits, change your lifestyle, put some little goals and try to achieve them because even the smallest achievement counts. Quitting smoking is an achievement, working out is an achievement. Applying for a job is an achievement. Especially when you decide to not give up no matter what. Even if the entire world is screaming « no you can't do it. » Show them what you are capable of. But the most important thing is to show it to yourself because you are only competing with yourself. Try every time to achieve a small goal without giving up. And after a period of time, you will realize that your entire life is changed and your problems are solved because this is how we change our lives. This is how we build a better life. Even the people who made great achievements started with many small achievements that we didn't see. Because we only see the rocket taking off and reaching the space, but we don't see the efforts, the fail, the trials, the patience and the fatigue.

Just like the chinese bamboo tree. Once you plant it, you need to water it, nurture it, and fertilize it daily. In its first year, we see no visible results. In the second year, no growth. The third, the fourth, still nothing. Our patience is tested because there is no evidence that your efforts are having any effects. And finally in the fifth year, the miracle. The chinese bamboo tree grown 80 feet in just six weeks. It dosn't mean the tree wasn't grown in the past four years. It was developping a strong unseen roots. What we learn from the story that we can work for a long period of time without any results. And suddently in just one day, you get surprised with the phenominal results that you didn't expect. So, never give up, always keep going, be optimistic and patient even with no results. What if these miserable tough years are making you stronger to prepare you for the big surprise. So, try again and again even with no results. You are already improving because strengh is something invisible and it takes time but growth is visible and it happens in just one second. And the bigger the strengh is, the higher the growth is. So, if you are strugeling a lot, get ready for the highest growth.

CONCLUSION :

« Do not grieve indeed God is with us. » « So verily with the hardship, there is relief. »

It's not this book who's going to change your life. It's a just a refreshment. It's you because you are already a fighter. You won a lot of inner battles that no one knows about : depression, anxiety, pain, loss, fear and you still alive. And you are still looking for ways to improve yourself. You should be proud of yourself because you are brave. You didn't end your precious life.

Now, close your eyes and try to take a deep breath. Imagine the air leaves with your stress and tension. Feel the peace and the calm. After that, you can go to action and be invincible. I also advice you to practice some meditation and good luck my friend.

www.ingramcontent.com/pod-product-compliance
Ingram Content Group UK Ltd.
Pitfield, Milton Keynes, MK11 3LW, UK
UKHW021934190726
13853UKWH00004B/1428

9 798516 261879